This too
SHALL PASS...

Ala Yvonne Kinlow Corbin

COPYRIGHT © 2024,

Publisher: Personal Freedom Publishing

Washington State.

ISBN# 978-0-9973994-7-9

All rights reserved. For information email:

vivian@viviangale.com

Dedication

This book is dedicated to my sister, Jeri and my daughter, Chelesa.

I am truly blessed as I watch you face, encounter and endure the many obstacles, pain, and tears that have been and continues to be in your way. Your faith and tenacity are a testament to all who know you.

I pray that as you reflect on days past, you will continue to lean into the One Who was there all the time and is the Source of your overcoming power.

Let the memory of how you overcame be your strength and encouragement, knowing that God is your always and forever Sustainer.

Because it came to pass!

You are living testimonies that Gods' strength is made perfect in human weakness.

You are blessed and highly favored. Not only are we family, we are friends… forever!

Preface

This is not a formula. It is an account that allows you to say "I believe I can make it!" Or even more so, "I know **I am** making it because I know there is Power and Love and Guidance and Compassion to steady me on my way." Real Life doesn't happen in a box; according to script.

Mrs. Corbin has provided an account of real life (the <u>simultaneous</u> crashes and victories) that allows the reader to hold their own whole-life experience intimately – rejecting none of it – and stand in confidence knowing that their own journey is valid and directed by a Loving Hand.

This is a book to feel as well as to read.

Nona Brazier
A forever friend and Teacher
Tyler, Texas

****

The Corbin's are valued and long-time friends to my wife, Deborah and myself. Their friendship throughout the years (many decades) is priceless. Yvonne writes from a deep-souled life journey of multiple hardships and struggles. The word 'experience,' contextually, means 'to be put to the test.' She shares prized and personal snippets of a life's journey that has indeed been tested. This coupled with remarkable resilience and overcoming conquests reveals outcomes of her and her family's perseverance.

This book shares her perspective of many of those battlefront clashes that often seemed too fierce to predict a positive result. However, the fortitude of a courageous and valiant believer/warrior matches the opposing operatives with incalculable weapons – often with strong crying and tears (Heb. 5:7) and the mighty strong-hold destroyers – that of prayer and the Word of God (2 Cor. 10:4).

Yvonne has a forthright and clear message that she has lived up to and her transparency has benefited a host of friends, families and both short and long-term acquaintances. Readers will find themselves caught in an atmosphere of tense anticipation as well as joyous reprieve. Her successes are not measured empirically by results and outcomes, but more so by quality of endurance, willful perseverance, and God-pleasing tenacity to scriptural disciplines and personal devotion.

Dr. Samuel Bass
A Pastor and Beloved friend
BSC Fellowship, Spanaway, WA

****

When Yvonne asked me to write this preface my first thought was, *"Lord, what would you have me say about your daughter?"* God gave me the verse John 13:35 NKJV.~ By this all will know that you are My disciples, if you have love for one another." Yvonne is a true disciple of Jesus. She loves Gods' people and seeing them come into the fullness of Christ. She beautifully shares her experiences, highs and lows bringing insight to the word and God's heart. Yvonne has many years serving in various positions in the Body. Her ministry is a bridge stretching across the divide and bringing the Body of Christ together. I have watched her minister to Gods' daughters in Mexico, singing over them and pouring into them in such love it brought me to tears.

The hardships of her life have not hardened her heart but drawn her closer to her Savior. Her first book *From Me to You,* she shares the real beginnings of her faith and love for Jesus. In this book she shares what God taught her going through the years in the in-between times or moments. She is full of wisdom and insights taught by the word through the Holy Spirit.
I am blessed to call her *'friend.'*

Pastor Jeanine Barnet,
A New Beginning Family Christian Center,
Gig Harbor, WA

****

Before becoming the wife of a pastor, I was a single working mom of 5. That in and of itself produced daily challenges. Along with that came lots of hurts and heartbreak. But after becoming a pastor's wife,

I had a new normal yet equally challenging life. It left me with very few people I could consider trustworthy with my heart outside of my husband. Yvonne has been one of those people that understood during both of these phases of my life.

As a leader of women's ministries for years, a mother of several offspring, a committed extended family member to her relatives and the wife of a husband that was severely injured on the job, Yvonne always found a way to rise to the challenge.

As you read her books, you will be able to relate to her journey *from tragedy to triumph*. She enlists scripture to make sense of any and every circumstance and still manages to be transparent and empathetic, unique and yet engaging. When you're at your lowest point there is a card in the mail, a text message, or a phone call, a visit or a gift.

She has the right to declare that life is full of ups and downs but indeed this too shall pass. Your experiences may be different, but you'll find yourself nodding in agreement as you read the process she has undergone. Follow her to a plausible conclusion. I have loved the privilege of calling her my friend.

Lady Deborah Bass, a devoted friend and co-pastor of BSC Fellowship, Spanaway, Washington State.

****

Acknowledgement

My heart felt gratitude to and for my family who have always supported me, and for sharing their voice in the story, *this is Real Life.*

Denise V, a dear and faithful friend, who, after reading my first book, "From Me to You," constantly challenged me and insisted that I write another book.

Lady Deborah Bass, who gave her time and talent to edit and format this book.

Philandra Eargle, a third-year student at DigiPen Institute of Technology in Redmond, Washington, and Vivian Gale for co-designing my cover.

Phil Eargle, a phenomenal photographer (Philandereaglephotography.com) and wonderful friend.

My niece, Vivian Gale, who without hesitation agreed to be my publisher.

To each of you who so graciously accepted my request to read my manuscript and give me a preface. I highly respect and appreciate each of you for your persona and the role you fulfill in my life.

To you, the reader, who also inspired me to pen this book.

Each of us experience seasons in life that we think will never end, and that we'll never make it through *this*.

As you read these short real-life experiences, be encouraged and strengthen in your inner man.

An old saying goes, *"Pick yourself up by your bootstraps"* and say, "I've come too far to quit now, this too shall pass!"

To God be the glory for Who He is, and, for the strength He continues to give us to complete our lifes' journey.

Contents

Copyright	ii
Dedication	iii
Preface	V
Acknowledgements	IX
Table of Contents	XI
This Too Shall Pass	12
Introduction	13
What is *This*?	16
Why?	21
In the Middle	26
Be an Overcomer	34
Inspiration	37
This is Real Life	42
Photos	53
Wait	55
When God When?	61
It Came to Pass	67
ADDENDUM	75
About the Author	79
Index	82

**This Too Shall Pass...**

Introduction

How often do we hear the phrase, *"This always happens," "It will always be this way,"* or *"it'll never end,"* etcetera.

We may have said these words ourselves!!!

My prayer is that as you read these pages you will be strengthened in your inner man, your faith will be renewed and you, too, will experience another facet of God's faithfulness and His grace. And that you will be inspired to start. To start again. To continue…

We experience seasons in life when we feel our inner self wondering, screaming; "WHAT? WHY? AGAIN?" Etcetera.

And sometimes these screams are in our outside voices.

Seasons were set in place by God when He created the earth, and they come to pass.
Day/night, Winter/Spring, Summer/Fall.

However, when we are in a season that is very traumatic and long, we can easily forget the one we just overcame.

The sooner we embrace and accept the inevitable, the sooner we will overcome *this* one too.

When I think of embrace, I think of many words of scripture in the Amplified Bible Version which reads; *"Trust in, rely on, lean on and be confident in."*

This is what I do as I continue to go from *this* to that, knowing that God is in control and regardless of the pain and the struggle, He is with me and will bring me through *this*, onward to my expected end.

It is hard to imagine that *this* is designed to make me strong, and I am to rejoice, be glad, and give thanks. REALLY???

Yes! We are to rejoice in the Lord and in everything give thanks.

The Lord is always worthy of our praise, and we give Him thanks for Who He is. Our Creator. The Author and Finisher of our faith. The more we know of His character, His love for us, and our love for Him, we can rejoice and give thanks because we have His promises, and as we trust Him. He will work it all out for our good and for His glory.

So, my friend, put on the whole armor, say as Jesus did in the Garden of Gethsemane, "If it be possible, let this cup pass; nevertheless, not *my will* but Thine be done." Gird up your loins; strengthen your spiritual, mental, and physical man and say to yourself "This too shall pass."

"And after you have suffered a little while, the God of all grace; Who imparts all blessings and favor; Who has called you to His own eternal glory in Christ Jesus, will Himself complete and make you what you ought to be, established and ground you securely, and strengthen, and settle you."
1 Peter 5:10 [AMP] Amplified Bible.

What is This?

"This," is what we wrestle with on any given day or what keeps us awake at night.

This comes in many different forms and in all stages of our lives. We may bring some of it upon ourselves; others may inflict it on us; it may be from satan or it may be something that God allows to bring us face to face with Him.

I have used *THIS* as an acronym to expound on some things that constitute challenges that we encounter.

T- things – Seek ye first the kingdom of God and all these things will be added unto you. (Matt.6:33 Amplified Bible.) Love not the world… the lust of the eye [craving and accumulating things, materialism], lust of the flesh [gratifying physical desires], pride of life [status]. (1 John 2:16, Amplified Bible.)

H- hurts – There is a Christ-Centered Recovery Program, (Celebrate Recovery), designed to help us with our hurts, hang-ups, and habits. I believe that our hurts can cause us to develop habits and hang-ups. Hurt has a way of going deep into our souls and if not ministered to, forgiven, and released, they can turn into resentment and bitterness. Hurt may also cause us to withdraw and become isolated.

Many times, we may forget the original cause of the hurt, however, the effect of the hurt remains and becomes poison in our personality.

I-insecurities- Insecurity is a feeling of inadequacy, not being good enough, and or uncertain. When uncertainty is present, we become unsure of who we are, forget Whose we are, and we can easily be deterred when we interact with other persons.

We can begin to compare ourselves with others (2 Cor. 10:12). Intimidation, other negative thoughts, and attitudes can make us lose our focus and we lose our self-worth which is in Christ Jesus, our Creator.

S-Self – however, on the other hand, we can become so sure of oneself that it is me, myself, I, my four and no more.

I am reminded of seven words from a former Senior Pastor Emeritus, that he gave me to expound upon when I was ordained in 2015.

As I re-read them now, I am encouraged to be aware of self and to keep an eye on the prize and what God has for me.

Those words are from 2 Timothy. And when the essence of these words become a part of ones' lifestyle, self will reflect the image and mirror of Christ.

- **Stir-up** the gift of God; many of us have been taught and seen examples of faith in God by one or more of our fore parents. It is up to us to rekindle, develop and move forward against the struggles that we are confronted with in life.
- As we live, society can challenge us to yield and or compromise the Gospel which we were taught. We are admonished to **hold** fast, to uphold the accuracy and integrity of the Gospel message.
- It is not always easy to remain steadfast- committed and faithful to God when the community in which we live conforms, at will, to the status quo. However, we must **endure-** persevere, remain in existence without yielding and denying our faith.
- The more I **study** and gain knowledge of God's Word, I am encouraged to **continue**

and maintain my walk with Him regardless of what comes my way. With God's Word hid in my heart, I am **watch**ful, alert and observant of worldly distractions and lusts that comes to shake my foundation.
- I **flee,** turn away from them with the power of Almighty God.

There will always be mountains to climb and valleys to cross, whether it is from within oneself or from the outside through relationships or society. However, it is important to remember that we are not responsible or accountable for what others may do or say, we are only liable for our response or reactions to them.

One or several of these may constitute a *this* is your life, but nonetheless, we are victors and not victims. We are more than conquerors through Jesus Christ our Savior and our Lord.

Encounters with Jesus always make the difference. Whatever challenges we may face, no matter the age or culture, even when we cannot see Him or feel Him. When we read His Word, believe, and walk by faith, and recall shared testimonies, we can know that I AM is with us. When we can't hear His voice, we continue to follow His plan, one day one moment at a time. Lord, this day, our daily bread.

WHY?

When things happen in life that we don't understand, it's hard to not ask the question, why me?

We have often heard the saying, *nobody told me that the road would be easy,* yet when it happens it's usually at a most inconvenient time, it's harder than we thought and lasts longer than expected.

We often become frustrated, angry, and resentful.

Must Jesus bear the cross alone and all the world go free? NO! there's a cross for everyone and there's a cross for me.

We are not expected to carry a wooden, two geometrical lines on our shoulders, we are to portray the true meaning of the cross; laying our lives down for others. That can be relishing my quiet time to listen to or doing an errand with or for someone. Loving one another, caring for each other as Jesus did in our everyday lives, as opportunity is presented.

"We are epistles of Christ, known and read of all men." See: (2 Corinthians 3:2). As epistles, we allow the gospel to be seen in our lifestyle, our everyday walk, not just in our talk. We persona God's goodness, glory, grace, mercy, and holiness.

We give more glory to God when we embrace our *this* in the midst of everyday life than when life is good.

Is it easy? No! But we have the promise of the Almighty with us, in us and alongside us, in the person of the Holy Spirit.

2 Cor 12:9 – And He said unto me, "My grace is sufficient for you. My strength is made perfect in weakness. Therefore, most gladly I will rather boast in my infirmities, that the power of Christ may rest upon me."

The first part of this verse was familiar to me. The latter part, when Paul said, "He will boast in his infirmities," was highlighted in my life during my husbands' tragedy in 1987. He was injured in a life-threatening accident at work with the chance of little or no survival: but God intervened. He's alive today.

A dear friend called me and said that God wanted me to embrace the latter part as we walked through his recovery.

And yes, it was a constant time of reflecting. We were in many different medical offices and each time, it seemed that we had to tell the story of what happened. I thought, *you have the file before you, read it!*

I heard God in my spirit say that although they saw him, the more they heard the story, it gave recognition and glory to the miraculous power of God. It changed my attitude!!! Amen

And ye shall be witness unto ME…our witness is most effective after we have had an encounter with Jesus Christ and the Holy Spirit lives inside of us.

In my early days, in church Y.P.W.W. (Young People Willing Workers), an evening Bible study on Sunday evenings, **our motto** was – *to be a representative of holiness in my everyday life and let my life be a mirror that reflects the image of God.*

We are ministers of reconciliation; (2 Corinthians 5:18). Our witness is to bring lost souls to Him and give strength and encouragement to the weak and weary.

In 2 Corinthians 1: 3,4 of the New King James Version (NKJV) in the Bible; Apostle Paul gives support to our suffering for the helping of others. It reads, "Blessed be the God and Father of our Lord Jesus Christ, the God of mercies and God of all comfort; Who comforts us in all our tribulation, that we may be able to comfort those who are in any trouble, with the comfort with which we ourselves are comforted by God."

We are to bear fruit, more fruit, and much fruit that will glorify God. (John 15).

In John 9:2, the disciples asked Jesus, "Who did sin, this man or his parents?" I always thought it strange that the question was asked, if the man sinned, seeing that he was blind from his birth. In verse 3, Jesus answered, that neither this man nor his parents, but that the works of God should be manifested.

Jesus was intentional when He waited to go to the town of Lazarus, in order that the glory of God may be revealed.

We may not ever know WHY some things happen while in this earth suit. And when we get to our eternal home, there will or *may be* no need to know. *Hallelujah*!

On our journey we have an Advocate Who understands our humanities and is more than able to carry us through to the other side.

When Jesus was on the cross, He cried, *My God, My God why have Thou forsaken me?*

He left His Divinity, took on humanity so that He could be our Advocate, our Intercessor, our Helper, and our Comforter as we encounter and as we travel life's journey.

And He is available today. He is right here, right now, to give you the endurance, the patience, grace, and mercy for your needs.

Bow your head, humble your heart, and ask Him! In Jesus name!

In the Middle

I am reminded of the poem entitled, "Dash," by Linda Ellis. It referred to the time between our birth and our death. What our life consisted of, our family, our profession, and our ministry.

It is the journey that takes place in the middle during our lifetime.

Examples...

> Sandwich: bread-condiments-bread
> Life: birth-everyday life-death
> Salvation- Holy Spirit – Eternity.
> It is the condiments in the sandwich that makes it complete.
> It is what happens between life and death that makes eternity a gain or a lost.

In my previous book "From Me to You," I wrote about "*In the Meantime*." The in-between time during the time between the beginning and the end. Note that the meantime can also be a mean time. A time when it seems like nothing is going right. A time span where it seems that things are standing still amid horror. However, that time is shaping and molding us for all that God has predestined for us. It is just a bridge that we are crossing over. It is just a season.

When we accept Salvation, it is the Holy Spirit Who walks with us through each challenge in our/ *this* journey. He is continually sanctifying us and making us ready for our eternal home.

I often say that I am in God's waiting room.

There will be many distractions, interruptions, delays, detours, and hurdles, pain, and tears.

During the global pandemic, *corona virus*, COVID-19, took the lives of millions, and shut down the economy worldwide. All people in the world were in God's waiting room.

During this time some of us at my local church are doing short weekly Facebook devotions to encourage our partners. Our themes were impactful, thought provoking and on-time for the season we were in.

Peace, Grateful, Resurrection Week, Rest, Unity, Chosen, Confidence, Contentment, Listening, and Wisdom.

Approximately two and a half months into the Pandemic, there was another crisis.

George Floyd, a black man was murdered by a white policeman holding his knee to his neck for over eight minutes, while three other policemen stood by. And all the while George was saying "I can't breathe."

Needless to say, this was *a mean*, meantime in our lives.

My husband and I were members in a multicultural non-denominational church where the pastor is Caucasian and where we served in leadership areas.

It was a very painful ordeal for us and many people of color in our congregation, especially when there was no immediate concern or prayer for the injustice that was done or any recognition and validation for the pain we were experiencing.

Even after Roy and I shared our hearts in a video and after a Black couple who were also in leadership and leaders in our community, did a Racial Equality 21- day Challenge, involvement from our Caucasian leaders was very limited.

Pastor S. who did the video is one who has a heart of compassion, and he has been a constant in our lives. Our relationship is becoming a friendship.

It makes me go… *"Humm, how am I valued, appreciated, and/or am I just a token to fill your minority platform??? OR…. Are they naïve to the emotional needs and care of others not like them? Do they not know how to address the issues? Are they reluctant to open their hearts and be vulnerable?*

I have the power of choice and I will prayerfully consider my options as I wait.

I must remember that it is for *this* that I have been chosen and not to move from my position or leave the waiting room because of *my* impatience.

Being contented will help me as I wait. Contentment, for me, is "An attitude that I learn as I continue this journey. (A learned intentional attitude of peace and satisfaction regardless of what I have or not and whatever is going on)." I must be intentional in knowing who and what God has for me, is for me. I must not allow myself to compare myself, my circumstances nor my surroundings with people or things that are around me.

Whereas, I must unite with other likeminded persons, I must continue to be me. It can be so easy to withdraw and or isolated during hard times, but it is then that we need others. Iron sharpens iron (Proverbs 27:17) and two are better than one…a three-string cord is not easily broken (Ecclesiastes 4:9-12).

Our commitment to remain in communion with God through Jesus Christ and to love Him with our whole mind, body, soul, and strength is a must.

This too can imply that I have encountered something that challenged me before. And as I remember that incident (s), how challenging it was and more so, how I overcame it, that will help me regain my strength, strengthen my faith, recharge my Spiritual battery, and give me courage to move forward.

Need I say that the year 2020 was a year second to none. Exhausting. More deaths were associated with Racial Injustice and more of the same – no compliances. We continued to hurt and walk alone, seemly without the support of our church family.

As a family, we experienced an unexpected painful tragedy; our 23-year-old grandson committed suicide.

That is a pain I do not wish anyone to have to experience. It is an on-going reality that we must face and learn to live with. Every day is an intentional choice to accept the things we cannot change, courage to change the things we can and the wisdom to know the difference. (The Serenity Prayer).

It is important to focus on the things we have, knowing that, as our daughter comforts herself with these words, *"God allowed it."*

I think of the Hebrew Boys in the fiery furnace, Daniel in the lions' den, and the things that Job suffered. After Job received the tragic news of his family, he bowed down and worshipped. God did not order these calamities; however, He allowed them and was with them throughout the journey.

Just as Jesus told His disciples, "Let's cross over to the other side," and was in the boat, however, He was asleep when the storm arose. The disciples were fearful and asked, "Do you not care that we are perishing?" However, when Jesus awoke, He calmed the storm. (Mark 4: 35-5: 1a)

Sometimes in our journey, it seems that Jesus is asleep, but even in the middle of our *this*, He is with us and will see us safely to the other side. When He speaks, His word is sure to come to fruition.

It is awesome that we have these witnesses who have gone before us, yet it is a painful journey. And I say journey because we see no destination in sight. It sounds good and works well in theory but in reality, it is a lonely and sad road to travel.

Facing the holidays, the pain is fresh, again.
The first holiday without him being there.
An empty place at the table; no sound of his laughter; no assistance as he helps prepare the meal.

I search for, look for, long for the comfort of my soul. Where do I turn? How can I find the strength to help my hurting child continue to face the reality of this loss.? How do I worship when my heart is heavy, weary, and worn?

I must, daily in the midst of my own sadness, look to the Hill from whence my help comes from.

In many of the Psalms, David shares encouragements that can help to strengthen our walk.

"In the multitude of my anxieties within me, Your [God] comfort delights my soul." Psalms. 94:19 NKJV;
My flesh and my heart fail; but God is the strength of my heart and my portion forever. Psalms. 73:26 NKJV.

Another chaotic scene for 2020!!

This is presidential election year! And the most complicated uncivilized, unnecessary one in all of history.

How can we move forward???
And an uprise with the corona virus.
Only the Lord knows, and He will continue to walk with us through it.

It is God's GRACE and MERCY that sustains us.

G – what He allows, we are to bring Him **Glory**
R- regardless of the storms, we will **R**EJOICE.
A – **A**lways abounding in Him.
C – even when we **C**RY, we are surrounded by His
E- **E**verlasting love.

M- He is **M**indful of us.
E- **E**veryday new mercies we see.
R – We have His **R**obe of **R**ighteousness.

C – He was **C**rucified that we may live.
Y – When we **Y**ield to His love, we will be overcomers of good and be victorious.

Just as the condiments in the middle make the sandwich, our Christian walk, our character, our trust and our faith are confirmed and solidified when we are in the middle of *this*.

So, don't despair or give up, let's continue to surrender to God; be filled with the Spirit; find a friend; hold fast to what we know and ask God to increase our faith. And continue to grant us His grace, and mercy toward us.

Be an Overcomer

Life is truly unpredictable, and we must be ready at all times to embrace the inevitable with God's grace, His mercy, and His love, so that whatever He says, our answer is *Yes Lord*. And it is better when we are surrounded with like-minded persons in Christian fellowships.

Being connected to a local *Body of Believers*, we are more apt to be accountability, responsible and committed.

We are familiar with the cliché, "It takes a village to raise a child," I submit that it takes a community to have a panoramic view of God. One race-human, with diverse ethnicities, cultures, gifts, and talents, but all with the same goal – Kingdom building.

Just as God instituted seasons, He did relationships.

Ecclesiastes 4:9-12 –Two are better than one…. for if they fall, one will lift up his companion…. and a threefold cord is not quickly broken.
Prov 27:17 – As iron sharpens iron, so a man sharpens the countenance of his friend. NKJV

To farther encourage relationships, He ordained, established, and laid the foundation for marriage. In Genesis 1:27, God made male and female.

Paul encouraged Spiritual relationships in Heb10:25 – not forsaking the assembling of ourselves together…but exhorting one another….

A person who overcomes is one who succeeds in dealing with or gain control of some problem or difficulty.

As followers of Christ, Overcomers, regardless of what we encounter, we hold fast to our faith in Christ.

It is through Him and the power of the Holy Spirit, that we are empowered to be effective in our lives and in our witness.

We continue pressing forward. We prevail to rise above the hardships we face. We endure until the end and finish the course. *In doing so…*

> We *must* have a relationship with God and a revelation of Who He is.
> We *must* worship.
> We *must* respect and love God's word.
> We *must* prioritize our life and live accordingly.

Through our relationship with Jesus Christ, we accept what He did on the cross for us, rely on His energy which is available to us through the Holy Spirit, and trust His Lordship regardless of what we see or feel. We must know that it is no surprise to Him and He has a plan already in place.

And we *must* receive and rest in His love for us.

The following is an insightful encouragement sent to me as an online devotional.

"My spiritual practices are the life raft that keeps me floating on top of the rough seas of life.

Time spent in prayerful contemplation, devotional reading, spiritual study, service, or fellowship, and *yes sending out the word,* keeps me tethered to my spiritual life,

These practices help remind me there is so much more to living than daily obligations and duties.
My relationship with God is my greatest comfort throughout all the seasons of life. It lifts me higher in easy times and keeps me from dipping too low in troubling times.

The more I focus my attention and energy on those activities and practices that draw me closer to God, the more I stay in the realm of comfort and support, no matter the state of my life or the world.

Inspiration

I will turn their mourning into joy, I will comfort them, and give them gladness for sorrow.—
Jeremiah 31:13

This is from a devotional calendar.
Happiness doesn't just happen. It isn't something we can sit around and wait to receive. It is not automatic, quite the opposite. We are fallen people living in a broken world and happiness is something we must be intentional about if we're to experience it. In many ways, happiness takes hard work.

It is important that we feed our spirit as well as our body to maintain a healthy and flourishing Christian lifestyle.

And our Christian relationships are just as important.

"This," is often overcome in our hearts and attitudes first and then a change occurs in our demeanor and lifestyle.

It may often leave a scar. However, I saw a Facebook post that read "Every scar that you have is a reminder not just that you got hurt, but that you survived."

We don't always understand or have the answers to our *this* but we have God's power and the word of Jesus to know that we came be overcomers.

St. John 16: 33 NKJV – Jesus said, "These things I have spoken to you, that in Me you may have peace. In the world you will have tribulations, but be of good cheer, I have overcome the world."

Reading the same passage of scripture in different versions, during different seasons can give different insights that are very uplifting and encouraging.

For example, Hebrews 13: 5b, 6 NKJV reads - for He Himself has said, I will never leave you nor forsake you. So, we may boldly say: "the Lord is my helper, I will not fear. What can man do to me?"

The Amplified Bible, reads- For He God Himself has said, I will not in any way fail you nor give you up nor leave you without support. I will not. I will not, I will not, not in any degree leave you helpless nor forsake nor let you down, relax My hold on you! Assuredly not.

So, we (I) take courage and are encouraged and confidently and boldly say, "The Lord is my Helper, I will not be seized with alarm; I will not fear or dread or be terrified; what can man do."

We are stronger and more consistent when we have persons in our life who are like minded.

When we develop activities- hobbies, exercise, journaling- that will help us maintain our focus, our purpose, and the pursuit of our goals.

Remember, God made us for relationships. Refuse to be alone. You may need to take the first step. Be aware of the person sitting next to you in worship.

One of my long ago forever friends is one who I stopped one Sunday and asked what was for dinner?

She and family lived just blocks from us. We often combined our dishes and made a complete meal. We both were a family of six.

Our lives have changed. We live in different states. However, our love and our friendship remain the same. We continue to share life together, our joys and our tears.

I am blessed to be in a natural family where love is personified. I am the youngest of eleven siblings. Only four of us are still alive. We are intentional with our relationship. We live in different states and are all over seventy-five years of age. As opportunity presents, we visit, and we have our scheduled conference calls.

We share, we laugh, we celebrate each other, and yes, we pray and cry together. We remember and honor our legacy. I am blessed and honored to be a part of this wonderful, loving, and God honoring family.

My family-n-love also gives me a panoramic view of God's blessings, love, grace and mercy.

Your *iron* maybe in your neighborhood; a senior; a single parent; in the marketplace.

Be aware and sensitive as to relationships that they are Divinely order. They maybe for a specific time and or for a specific reason. And yet, some maybe for a lifetime. However, that relationship may be more intimate during times of need and different seasons of life.

Ask God to lead you as you go, and He will.

This is Real Life

I asked my family to share a *this* moment …

One of my husbands' sayings is, "One thing for sure in life is change," and we must adjust to it.

And if anyone knows, it is him.

This is a *this* from my husband, *Roy*.

"I was in a traumatic industrial accident 30+ years ago that changed my life forever.

I was totally unaware of my injuries; I just knew that I had a horrific headache. I immediately fell on my knees and said "Lord, help me." And I'm here today because He did and He keeps on doing, just that.

My wife was at church when she got the news. She immediately told the group of the emergency and came to the hospital. Upon arrival, she was told of the seriousness, and she called back to the church and within moments, some went into prayer and others flooded the hospital chapel.

The hospital medical team waited most of the night before they decided to operate because they said I would not live. But God.

After many operations and medical treatments, I was able to establish some of normality.

I had a wife and three children to care for (our oldest was married and in Germany).

I have not had an 8am-5pm employment schedule since then. Once my health became stable, I looked for opportunities to be active.

I reconnected with familiar relationships and started investing in our community.

I became a volunteer mentor with an organization called "Homework Connection," that helped multicultural students after school.

I was a volunteer at one of our Middle Schools until the Pandemic.

I am still a volunteer at one of our Food Network Outreaches to help meet needs.

During the early years with this outreach, we were also connected with Toys for Tots during the Christmas holidays. I especially have a passion to help the homeless.

Although the major trauma passed, there were ongoing life alterations that made our family life quite different. I continue to live with them every day. And every day, new mercies I see!" ... ***Roy***

From my children...

"This song, *Firm Foundation* by Maverick City, is perfect for what we are facing with our children and the chaos of the world.

Father, we do not know the why You chose us for this journey with our children and families, but we know there is a testimony somewhere down the road even though it may seem hard to see right now.

The journeys have been long and sometimes frustrating, but we don't give up. We are holding on because Your Word doesn't return void and your Promises are yes and amen. Plus, we've raised them the way You said, and we know they have to be okay because they can't run and depart forever. Keep them close to You, God and draw them even if they do not realize it.

They are going to be okay because You are the Maker of them, and Your hands are the most capable to handle all their hurts, voids, insecurities, and questions they don't understand. Be with them and keep them safe." ***Cassandra***

"Have you ever thought about your life like a puzzle? ❧ Before now, I hadn't made a literal comparison. During this *safer-at-home* period, I pulled out some puzzles to fill some time. After I began working on the recent one, I received an inspirational message.

There are so many pieces to a puzzle, and each piece is unique though many of them closely resemble. Just 'one' tiny difference will prevent a perfect fit and the picture will be skewed if a single piece is incorrectly placed.

I start with the straight edges to complete the border since that's the easiest part. Moving on to the inside, I attempt to finish one section at a time. As I pick up different pieces hoping for a fit the results vary. One piece was too loose and left a crack.

The next one isn't the right blue hue and the opening is on the wrong side. Another piece kinda fits, but I had to force it.... too snug. Growing impatient and ready to be done, I'd stop, consider the many options on the table and patiently look again.

Ahhhh, I think this is it.... the right coloration, the right size, the perfect shape and all openings look on point. YES, it fits! Then I got down to the end only to find missing pieces.... Ugh! ☹ That was not "my plan."

Life in Christ can be a puzzle. We all have unique characteristics and different paths we can choose to take. Our body is the outside border; we must take care of our temple. See: (I Timothy 4:8).

What about the inside; the inner parts? Trying to figure out those parts and make the right decisions for our life can be a monster. When put together, these pieces affect the picture of our life. Some basic factors are what we eat, drink, or otherwise ingest; our thoughts, feelings, emotions, what we watch and read, what job to take, who to date/marry, how to raise our children, where to live.... the list goes on. These are "pieces" to our life's puzzle.

It's not always easy to figure out how to put them together, but we can turn to "The Word". It isn't about *our* plan; rather it's "GOD'S divine purpose and PLAN" for our lives that we want accomplished. Just as there are missing pieces in the puzzle that I searched for and couldn't find, there is SPACE in our LIFE that ONLY JESUS CAN FILL. No matter what we do or how hard we try, nothing else will work.

Jer 1:5 (NLT) - "I KNEW you BEFORE I formed you..."

Prov 3:5-6 - "TRUST in the Lord with all thine heart....in ALL thy ways...."

James 1:2-4 (NKJV)- "My brethren, count it all joy.... the testing of your FAITH produces PATIENCE..."

Jer 29:11 (MSG) - "I KNOW what I'm doing. I have it all planned out—plans to take care of you, not abandon you, plans to give you the future you hope for."

ALLOW Christ to provide the missing pieces and fill the empty spaces in your lives. He can do it better than we ever could. 🙏😇 *Chelesa*

I enlisted into the Marine after graduating from High School. It was while being stationed in Japan that my life took a radical turn.

Although many tragedies occurred within our family during my teenage years (near tragic accident involving my father, death of my first nephew), it was in Japan when I had no family support and was unable to return home during a major accident which killed my cousin, my godbrother and a close friend, I was at a loss. It was then that alcohol became my go-to companion.

I've been addicted to alcohol, sex, porn, self-gratification, anger, and murderous thoughts! All of this because I thought I was a man, could skip reading GODS word every day, not be consistent in my *prayer life* and could do it alone without Men mentors and No accountability.

I actually thought I LOVED people until the HOLY SPIRIT gut checked me and showed me, I didn't even LOVE myself, so how could I LOVE others who were created by our FATHER?

I'm in my 50's now and the HOLY SPIRIT put me in my place in my mid-40s.

What a wakeup call to realize I was still empty after giving my life to CHRIST at 28 years old!

Although I've had good mentors in my life, my life became more complete and transforming when I started going to L. C. Church in Tacoma, WA. I finally invested and got connected to a GOD centered Men's group that was very open, honest, vulnerable, and accountable to JESUS first, and to each other!

A good Friend and brother named Steven L. helped me over some hurdles through sharing some of his struggles with me and asked the group, "are You Hot or cold for CHRIST?" I thought for a couple seconds and told myself, sometimes I'm Hot and sometimes I'm cold. The HOLY SPIRIT whispered, "that's Lukewarm," (Revelations 3:16)!!! I began to change right there in the classroom because I felt Convicted, not condemned.

I'm accountable to GOD plus some Strong and Straight forward Men and Women who hold me to HIS standards and not the worlds' because I choose to Surrender to JESUS daily.

No, I'm not Perfect but I am on the right track to become more like our SAVIOR as I live one day at a time. It's Never a One and done thing with Spiritual growth in becoming a True Man who LOVES GOD, it is a journey I want to take.

You can Never defeat Satan on your own power because he knows your weak spots and how to tempt you or distract you from drawing closer to JESUS.

It will take moment by moment Surrender just to get through one day, and at the end of that day, thank GOD, you made it that far and Never give up!

Always Surrender to PERFECT LOVE, JESUS CHRIST. In daily Surrender of your old self, *it too* shall pass." ***Calveo***

"So......... I got up Saturday morning trying to figure out what I was going to wear, and I felt pressed to wear one of my nephews', R'Jais' t-shirts. As I'm getting my clothes together something was tugging at me to wear one of my brothers' t-shirts instead, so I did.

I'm going about my day and while I'm at the nail shop I pick up my phone and see that my sis Destiny tagged me in something, so I check it out and then it hits me, and I realize the *actual date*....... it's my brother, Lafayette R Dorsey Sr. birthday. Y'all, all I knew was that it was Saturday and that was all I was paying attention to.

When I tell you I'm in the nail shop trying to keep my composure, I really mean that! Cuz, it hits me all over again that my brother isn't here. At the same time, I felt comfort because he was reaching out to me and giving me some love. I ended my day having a chat with my Chesapeake and all was right again. Laf, I think of you and R'Jai so many times throughout the day, EVERY SINGLE DAY, and I have to remind myself that you're together and in a better place.

I'm low-key still, kinda mad at you cuz I got that vaccine so I could come see you and you left anyway 😒😒. Antyhoo…, ALWAYS AND FOREVER in my heart and I will continue to carry you both with me every single day until I join you."
Consuella~

"I am thankful for my family. We have gone through many hard heart aches.

Sometimes together and sometimes apart, we do not live in the same city nor state.

Technology makes it possible to stay connected physically even though we are always connected in our hearts.

We are not able to share each detail at times, yet we can share our hurt, our pain, our love, our prayer, and yes, our victories. And…… our tears, losses, and disappointments.

We don't always agree or understand the choices that one may make, however we are a family with different personalities and different assignments from our Heavenly Father.

Communication and patience are important, especially as a parent. As we navigate through our differences becoming the family that God intends us to be, we continue to move forward, share, and show His love to bring glory to His name, even during and through the hard times.

As parents, no matter the age of our children, we get the opportunity to be in God's Waiting Room while He's preparing our children to be all He predestined them to be. And we, parents get to grow in wisdom and grace. All the while, God is still growing us.

Life very seldom goes the way we plan, expect, or wish it to be, yet in the midst of chaotic events, everyday life continues, and we must choose how we let it affect our day.

With God's help, we have overcome the traumatic accident of Roy, the death of our first grandson, juvenile diabetes, emotional disorders, suicide attempt, the suicide of one grandson, the death of a son-in-love, two divorces, four grands out of wedlock and Cancer.

And through it all, we have four college graduates through three generations, Community Activists, a

Real Estate Agent in two different states, a Financial Accounts Processor for a nation-wide food chain, a Retired Loan Officer and now an Executive Pastor, a Buyer, for a local restaurant and Small Business Owner, and much more.

God is faithful in every generation and in every season.

We are a happy family with four children, six grands and one great grand.

I'm here to encourage you that there's always a song, a word, a voice to help you continue; to show you the correct puzzle piece for the right spot.

I encourage you to be the part of the body who will inspire and encourage others to grow and fulfill their call.

HE, (God), makes the whole body (family) fit together perfectly. As each part does its own special work, it helps the other parts grow, so that the whole body (family) is healthy and growing and full of love. Ephesians 4:16 New Living Translation.

Always remembering that we are on a journey…together…
…and *this* too will pass.

We are family. Christmas 2023!

Wait

So, I...

W A I T

And that, my friend, can be easier said than done.

It does not matter how much I may want it NOW, I'm reminded that my times are in HIS hands. (Psalm 31:15)

My life, my every moment, my destiny- it's all in Your hands. (*Psalm 31:15a*, Passion Translation Bible)

I am challenged again, to evaluate my level of trust and confidence in God....

I continue to choose daily (sometimes, moment by moment), to trust Him.

That may be the reason Jesus taught His disciples to pray, "give us this day our daily bread" and why the children of Israel had to gather manna daily.... Jesus also told us "To take up your cross DAILY and follow ME."

Our waiting is not finding a comfy chair and folding our arms. It is an attitude of trust and confidence as we go about our daily tasks.

Waiting can also be likened to pregnancy; many unexpected things may happen between conception and delivery; however, we continue with the pregnancy, unless the unfortunate occurs and the baby is aborted, until our expected due date. We may even experience a time when we feel like it's time, only to hear the doctor say, "not yet." Remember, our times are in His hands.

Sometimes to avoid abortion, there may be a need to have complete rest for a span of time.

We may also need to have rest while in God's waiting room. In the waiting, things happen!

He may call us to reset some boundaries, let go of some things and activities that we hold dear, and yes, some relationships.

The waiting room can be a lonely and an alone time.

There have been times when I really felt that I needed to share with a physical person, lol, but I couldn't. No one answered their phone; they were busy, or they thought I was strong enough to conquer. Or my spirit just said wait. And in doing so, through the emotional struggle, God ministers to my spirit.

I also find it helpful for me to reach beyond myself. I send a text, a card, an email, or walk across my yard and chat with a neighbor.

I enjoy adult coloring, on my phone and in a coloring book. I find the coloring book is more engaging than my phone when I really need to refocus. The book challenges me to choose what color to put where. The phone gives the color instructions.

We can easily become depressed and withdraw while waiting.

So instead, look for options that will help you remain faithful and be your authentic self.
Be who God called you to be before you were in your mothers' womb.

Many times, my mind says yes but my emotions and motivation say no. However, when I push past those, my feelings change and I'm better.

Engage in a hobby. Find opportunities to serve in your community and in your Christian family.

As I was feeling a bit weary one day, I heard in my spirit, portions of the scripture, Jeremiah 17:8 – be not anxious in the year of drought, [a prolonged absence of a specified thing. Dryness.] ye shall still bear fruit.

That complete scripture reads, beginning with verse 7 – "Blessed is the man who trusts in the Lord, and whose hope is in the Lord. For he shall be like a tree planted by the waters, which spreads out its roots by the river, and will not fear when heat comes, but its leaf will be green, and will not be anxious in the year of drought, nor will crease from yielding fruit." NKJV.

In Jesus' humanity while He was dying on the cross, He still bore fruit. He gave life to one of the thieves on the cross (Luke 23:43) and He acknowledged and made accommodations for His Mom. (John 19:26-27).

We can lose **W**eights. Things that can easily cause us to become distracted.

Our **A**ttitudes can be rearranged; we can become more, …

Intuitive and sensitive to God's plan for our lives and be, …

Teachable to adhere and apply needed changes to our lifestyle.

Paul exhorted Timothy to fight the good fight of faith, (1 Tim. 6:12)

To fight is to engage in a struggle, a battle, some sort of combat and/or attack.

And we know that in our journey, our fight is not with humanity nor is it with natural weaponry. (Ephesians 6:12). Our fight is against the powers of darkness.

Paul talks a lot about his fight in his letters to the Corinthians' church. (2 Corinthians 6:1-10). And he declared his valedictory in 2 Tim. 4:7 "I have fought the good fight; I have finished the race…"

That, my friend, is what we all want to say and hear our Father say, "Well done, good and faithful servant, enter in."

When we stay connected to the Holy Spirit and read His Word, we are more able to trust the process and maintain our faith.

Yes, while in the waiting room!

I read these words in the commentary, "With the Word: by Warren Wiersbe; "True faith is not in a hurry; it is willing to wait".

Psalm 31: 24b Passion Translation Bible – "Wait for Him to break through for you, all who trust in Him. God is faithful!"

Psalm 16:8b, Passion Translation Bible – "My confidence will never be weakened for I experience Your *wraparound* presence every moment."

In our waiting, we may get weary, and we may experience fear. There may be times when we say, . . .

"WHEN?
GOD
WHEN???"

Have you experienced waiting in the doctors' office? After sitting in the waiting area for a long time, you're finally called into a room, only to wait some more. The nurse comes in and takes your vitals and you wait again. Finally, in comes the doctor!

Regardless of how long it takes and how many challenges we encounter, our wait is not in vain. Even in our waiting, God is with us.

In 2019 many things happened and changed the course of history forever.

The Pandemic… the virus that shut down the world The death of many persons of color.

Our unfair judicial system, [and the lack of support from our Christian Family (Multicultural Leadership)].

Our grandsons' suicide.

Within a year of our grandsons' death, his mom, our daughter was diagnosed with Breast cancer. And if that wasn't enough, his dad was diagnosed with Stomach cancer. (He transitioned in 2022.)

Let's not even mention the many deaths and unhealthy diagnosis that occurred during this time. Just in the month of January, 2022, our family experienced four deaths, one including my oldest sibling.

As I was meditating some time ago, trying to get perspective and move forward, this portion of scripture was highlighted to me.

In the Passion Translation Bible, 1 Peter 5: 6,7 – "If you bow low in God's awesome presence, He will eventually exalt you as you *leave the timing in His hands*. Pour out *all* your worries and stress upon Him and *leave them there*, for *He always tenderly cares for you.*"

1 Peter 5:7b AMP reads…He cares for you affectionately and cares about you watchfully.

As I continue on this journey, I'm often wondering "When will this season change and be over?"
Will it ever be, or will I feel normal again?
What is normal anyway? Hummm! Is this it? Is this the precursor of the end times?

Matthew 24:6a, 7 NKJV– "And ye shall hear of wars and rumors of wars…for nation will rise against nation and kingdom against kingdom, and there will be famines, pestilences, and earthquakes in various places."

2 Timothy 3;1 ESV- "But understand this, that in the last days there will come times of difficulty."

NKJV 3:1b – "But know this, that in the last days perilous times will come."

In the midst of these disasters and calamities, I know God has a purpose and a plan, yet in the flesh, we continue to look for them to pass.

So, what are we to do?
Pray - Wait - Be patient - Maintain our faith - Don't waver -Be confident - WAIT.

Is it always easy? **NO!**

It is an everyday, constant choice.
As *I keep my heart set on the things above,* as (Colossians 3:2 encourages). I hear encouragements all around.

Just now on Daystar TV station, I hear "He is a Sustainer."

God's Word is here for our empowerment.
Even when we don't know how to pray or have words to say.

Roman 8:26 in the Easy Read Bible, reads – "Also, the Spirit helps us. We are very weak, but the Spirit helps us with our weakness. We don't know how to pray as we should, but the Spirit Himself speaks to God for us. He begs God for us, speaking to Him with feelings too deep for words."

That same verse in the Passion Translation Bible reads – "The Holy Spirit takes hold of us in our human frailty to empower us in our weakness." For example, at times we don't even know how to pray, or know the best things to ask for. But the Holy Spirit rises up within us to super-intercede on our behalf, pleading to God with emotional sighs, too deep for words.

I love these versions! Don't you? Thank You Holy Spirit!

Yet, we can still agonize as to *when*.

His delays are not always denials.

Someone sent me a text message which read, "Not all storms come to disrupt your life; some come to clear your path."

Another one reads, "Sometimes God closes doors because it's time to move forward. He knows we won't move unless circumstances force us to."

And if they are denials, it's because He has a better plan. WAIT!

Yes, I get weary, frustrated, and many times, feel stuck; but I realize, feelings are not my reality, Gods' Word, and my relationship with Him, are. And the more I spend time with Him and know His character, my waiting is softened with His presence.

Another encouragement – Psalm 31: 24 Passion Translation Bible;

"So, cheer up! Take courage, all you who love Him. wait for Him to break through for you, all who trust in Him!"

Every day is "Lord, this day, my daily bread." Every night, "Thank You, Lord for one more day."

I'm sure you've heard the acronym for fear- False Evidence Appearing Real.

Let's turn our fear into FAITH. I found an acronym that I like for faith – FOREVER ALWAYS I TRUST HIM. He is the Good Shepherd and His character and reputation are flawless, and He's only a prayer away.

1 Peter 5:10 English Standard Version- "And after you have suffered a [little] while, the God of all grace, Who has called you to His eternal glory in Christ, will Himself restore, confirm, strengthen, and establish you."

Jude 24,25 KJV – "Now unto Him that is able to keep you from falling and to present you faultless before the presence of His glory with exceeding joy, to the only wise God our Savior, be glory and majesty, dominion, and power, both now and ever. Amen.

In the meantime, I continue to trust in His timing, worship, and be strengthened.
How about You?

It Came to Pass
this too **SHALL** pass.

We are in the world together sharing and traveling through our own "this"; how blessed we are that we have the Father, the Son, and the Holy Spirit with us.

There are many scriptures that read, "and *it came to pass* when; it came to pass *after*; it came to pass *that;* it came to pass *at the end*;" etc.

So, is it possible that our "this" is on-hold until we *do that?*

…...and what could *that* be?

I'm glad you asked….

Have I surrendered my all to God?

Is He my Lord and Savior or do I want Him just as my Savior?

And what is the difference???
When He is Lord, I honor Him in all areas of my life. I love Him with my heart, soul, mind, and strength.

As my Savior, I call on Him when I need some special act or deliverance.

Do I look for His hand or for His face? His providences, what I get from Him or Who He is?

When I cast my cares, do I leave them?

When my out-go is greater than my income...

When I continue to eat unhealthily...

Then will I hear from heaven....

Yes, times can be mean, but with God, we can make it.

Jesus told us in St. John 16:33b, "In the world you will have tribulation, but be of good cheer, I have overcome the world."

St. John 14: 27, NKJV- "Peace I leave with you, My peace I give to you, not as the world gives do I give to you. Let not your heart be troubled, neither let it be afraid. [AMP-... stop allowing yourselves to be agitated and disturbed; and do not permit yourselves to be fearful and intimidated and cowardly and unsettled]."

Paul warned us again in 2 Timothy 3 that in the last days *perilous times will come* and he encouraged us in Galatians 6: 9, *to not grow weary while doing good.* And in 1 Cor 15:58, *to be steadfast, immoveable always abounding in the work of the Lord, knowing that our labor is not in vain in the Lord."*

Chapter 16: 13, "Watch, stand fast in the faith, be brave, be strong."

"After we have suffered a little while, the God of all grace, Who has called you to His eternal glory in Christ, will Himself restore, confirm, strengthen and establish you." 1 Peter 5:10 *NASB*, New American Standard Bible.

This is possible when we are in daily communication with the Father, Son, and Holy Spirit and when we get dressed in the Whole Armor……

We can choose to become bitter or to become better.

We can choose faith, trust, and hope in God or our feelings and our sight by what we see.

When we choose faith, this is our confidence….
Now to Him Who is able to keep you from stumbling and to present you blameless before the presence of His glory with great joy, to the only God, our Savior, *through* Jesus Christ our Lord, be glory, majesty, dominion, and authority, before all time and now and forever. Amen. Jude 24, English Standard Version.

"The Lord bless you and watch, guard, and keep you; the Lord make His face to shine upon and enlighten you and be gracious (kind, merciful, and giving favor to you; the Lord lift up His

[approving] countenance upon you and give you peace (tranquility of heart and life continually)."
Numbers 6: 24-26 AMP Version.

So, my friend, stay in the fight.
Remember, *this too shall pass!*

However, keep *the Whole Armor on,* because God is still preparing us for our expected end.

The Whole Armor protects us from head to toe…
the Belt of Truth; the Breastplate of Righteousness; Sandals of the Gospel of Peace; Shield of Faith; Helmet of Salvation: Sword of the Spirit.

When we are dressed properly, in God's Armor, we are able to win any and every battle!

"Be anxious for nothing but in everything by prayer and supplication with thanksgiving, let your requests be made known to God; and the *peace of God* which *surpasses* all understanding, will *guard* your hearts and mind *through* Christ Jesus." Philippians 4:6,7 NKJV.

Gods' peace is quiet, confident, and trusting regardless of circumstances.

His peace surpasses, it exceeds, it's greater than any other. It guards our hearts, in order to protect us against damage or harm.

It is in and through the things that Christ Jesus suffered, endured, and overcame, that we are able to overcome whatever challenges and obstacles that come our way. (John 16:33)

It Came to Pass!

ADDENDUM

As I stated earlier, this is one of the worst seasons of my life. It seems to be an on-going emotional, mental, and spiritual roller-coaster journey with no end in sight.

There has been some justice executed in the judicial system.

We have found a place to worship, the presence of God and His Word are there. After attending Sunday worship for two years, we decided to take the next step and attend Membership Class.

Although, we are not in Leadership Ministry as we have been accustomed to, we are definitely in pew ministry, getting to know and connecting with those who are in the pews around us. And getting to know more about the culture and its Kingdom call. So, we worship!

We went to Los Angeles to visit our daughter in February 2023 for two weeks, only to be there until after Mother's Day. Our son-in-love who was battling stomach cancer transitioned on March 29th. His mom also transitioned February 10th and her memorial was March 9th. He was not able to attend her service.

So, we stayed to be with our daughter through her first holiday without him, especially because it was Mother's Day.

Soon after his death, she had many other important days without him. Father's Day, their daughters' college graduation, and his birthday.

We have a circle of family and friends who continue to share life with us. It was during this time that we experienced just how important family and friends are. We had tremendous support. Not only did we get calls, texts, and cards, we had many to travel from far and near to share the pain and the tears with us. We also share with others in their *this*. Life flows better in community, especially when we are traveling in the same direction with the same goal.

When I think I'm ready to get back in the race of life and regain normality, there is *this* again. I realize that every day I must choose to rejoice and be glad and content in whatever state of being I'm in. Not necessarily in the *this,* but in the One Who is in control of it all, Christ Jesus my Savior and Lord.

I may feel helpless but *Never* hopeless!

I pray that you are reading this in the spirit in which it was written and that you are being encouraged and strengthened as your story is still being written.

Each day is a new day and another opportunity to say, "Yes Lord, I surrender to Your plan for my life".

W E L L ... as it is that this book is not completed, I must add another *this*.

It is February 2024, and we are getting ready to experience and relive the memories of the journey of saying goodbye for now, (we look forward to seeing you in glory) to our son -in-love.

It was another month of firsts. Their 31st anniversary and Valentine's Day, without him.

My grandsons' phrase was "God's got me".
My son-in-loves' phrase was "Live in the moment."

My daughter, Chelesas' phrase was "God allowed it to happen."

At any unpredictable moment, one or all of these phrases may come to mind. Sometimes I can smile, and say, "I agree", other times, they may make my heart bleed and I have to have my own phrase...

"My flesh and my heart fail; But God is the strength of my heart and my portion forever."
Ps.73:26

When I stay close to my Anchor, the pain is there, however, the sting is not as deep. The tears still flow but not as a stream.

What is your go-to when your heart is weary? Your secret place? A song? A scripture?

Keep the *yes* alive in your heart regardless of the season you are in, and the God of hope will be right there with you. Maybe not as soon as you wish; not like you wish; however, He's always there.

When I feel my heartbeat, I realize, yes, He's here! And I recall the lyrics to a song, "Spirit of the Living God, fall fresh on me".

Say as Jesus said in the Garden of Gethsemane, "Nevertheless, *Your will* be done." (Luke 22;42)

Because IT came to pass.

About the Author

Ala Yavonne Kinlow Corbin,
is an overcomer of many of life's
obstacles.

She is better known as Yvonne.
Yvonne, was born in Dumas, Arkansas to the late Reverand Ezra Dewitt Kinlow and Mrs. Mary Kinlow and is the youngest of 11.

She moved to Tacoma, Washington in 1966 with her husband Roy Corbin.

Her certification and experience in Human Services includes …

A college graduate from Evergreen State College. Counseling from IBET, A Christian Institute.

A mentor and facilitator to women, youth, and marriage events.

Yvonne was a business owner for more than 20 years. A Director of a multicultural after school program, Homework Connection.

Founder of S.H.E. Ministries (Sharing Holistic Experiences), A support group for women, and an Associate Pastor in a non-denominational, multicultural congregation.

She enjoys sharing Biblical and godly principles through her lifestyle of worship with those she meets.

She resides in Federal Way, Washington with husband, Roy, of 57 years. They have 4 grown children, 6 grands, 1 great grand.

She is also the author of "<u>From Me to You</u>".

To contact the Author, send email to:

<u>ayvonnecorbin@comcast.net</u>

Index

AGAIN..................... 13
ALWAYS 50, 65
An old saying goes, "*Pick yourself up by your* x
Armor............... 69, 70
attitude 23, 29, 56
attitudes.............. *17, 37*
Attitudes.................. *58*
becoming *vii, 28, 48, 51*
believer.....................*vi*
Bible*14, 15, 23, 38, 55, 59, 62, 64, 65*
blessed..... *iii, vii, 39, 67*
brought ....*vii*
Business *52*
chaotic *32, 51*
character...... *14, 33, 65*
children *43, 44, 46, 51, 52, 55, 80*
Christ..... *vii, 15, 17, 18, 19, 22, 23, 29, 35, 45, 47, 65, 69, 70, 71, 74*
church... *23, 27, 28, 30, 42, 59*
compare.............. *17, 29*
complete..*x, 15, 26, 39, 45, 48, 56, 58*
condemned *48*
conference *39*
connecting *73*
continue..*iii, 13, 14, 18, 19, 29, 31, 32, 33, 35, 39, 43, 50, 51, 52, 55, 56, 62, 63, 66, 68, 74*
count......................... *46*
countenance *34, 70*
courage *30, 38, 65*
Creator............... *14, 17*
crisis *27*
cross *19, 21, 24, 31, 35, 55, 58*
Dash *26*
daughters ....*vii, 74*
decisions................... *45*
denials *64*
depressed.................*57*
destiny *55*
difference ... *19, 30, 45, 67*
different *viii, 16, 23, 38, 39, 40, 43, 45, 51, 52*
disciple ....*vii*
disciples..*vii, 24, 31, 55*
distractions *19, 27*
Divinity *24*
earth................... *13, 24*
easier *55*
eat...................... *46, 68*
embrace *14, 22, 34*

employment *43*
encouragement .. *iii, 23, 36, 65*
enter *59*
established *15, 34*
experience .. *v, x, 13, 30, 37, 56, 59, 60, 75, 79*
experiences .... *vii, viii, x*
experiencing *28*
faith ... *iii, vii, 13, 14, 18, 19, 30, 33, 35, 58, 59, 63, 65, 69*
family . *iii, vi, viii, ix, 26, 30, 39, 40, 42, 43, 47, 50, 51, 52, 57, 62, 74*
feelings . *46, 57, 64, 65, 69*
fight *58, 59, 70*
flawless *65*
flesh *16, 32, 63, 75*
forget**Error! Not a valid bookmark in entry on page** 13, 13, 17
forsake *38*
forthright .... *vi*
friendship .... *v, 28, 39*
frustrated *21, 65*
glory . *x, 14, 15, 22, 23, 24, 51, 65, 66, 69, 75*
goal *34, 74*
God .. *iii, vi, vii, x, xi, 13, 14, 15, 16, 18, 19, 22, 23, 24, 27, 29, 30, 32, 33, 34, 35, 36, 38, 39, 40, 42, 44, 51, 52, 55, 56, 57, 58, 59, 61, 62, 63, 64, 65, 66, 67, 68, 69, 70, 73, 75, 76*
GRACE *32*
growing *51, 52*
Hallelujah *24*
hands *44, 55, 56, 62*
happens *13, 21, 26*
hard . *14, 21, 29, 37, 44, 46, 50, 51*
hardened .... *vii*
hear . *13, 19, 56, 59, 62, 63, 68*
heart . *vii, viii, ix, 19, 25, 28, 31, 32, 46, 50, 63, 67, 68, 70, 75, 76*
heavy *31*
hold ..... *v, vi, 18, 33, 35, 38, 48, 56, 64, 67*
holiday *31, 73*
Holy Spirit *64*
hurts .... *vii, 17, 44*
imply *29*
important *19, 30, 37, 51, 74*
inner .... *x, 13, 45*
Insecurity *17*
Inspiration .... *xi, 37*
intentional ... *24, 29, 30, 37, 39*
intimately .... *v*

isolated *17, 29*
Jesus *vii, 14, 15, 17, 19, 21, 23, 24, 25, 29, 31, 35, 38, 55, 58, 68, 69, 70, 71, 74, 76*
Job *30*
journey *v, viii, x, 24, 25, 26, 27, 29, 30, 31, 44, 48, 52, 59, 62, 73, 75*
kingdom *16, 63*
Kingdom *34, 73*
know .... *iii, v, vi, 14, 19, 24, 28, 30, 33, 35, 38, 44, 59, 63, 64, 65, 73*
life .. *v, vii, viii, ix, x, 13, 17, 18, 19, 21, 22, 23, 25, 26, 35, 36, 38, 39, 40, 42, 43, 44, 45, 47, 48, 51, 55, 58, 64, 67, 70, 73, 74, 79*
LIFE *46*
Living *52, 76*
lonely *31, 56*
Lord .. *vi, 14, 19, 23, 32, 34, 38, 42, 46, 58, 65, 67, 68, 69, 74*
Love .... *v, 16*
man .... *x, 13, 15, 24, 27, 34, 38, 47, 58*
manages .... *viii*
Meantime *26*

mercies *23, 32, 43*
ministry .... *vii, 26, 73*
molding *27*
monster *45*
mountains *19*
must *18, 29, 30, 31, 34, 35, 36, 37, 42, 45, 51, 74, 75*
nodding .... *viii*
occurred *47, 62*
overcome *14, 37, 38, 51, 68, 71*
Pandemic *27, 43, 61*
patience *25, 51*
perfect ...... *iii, 22, 44, 45*
phone ..... *viii, 49, 56, 57*
piece *45, 52*
poem *26*
policeman *27*
possible .. *14, 50, 67, 69*
practices *36*
prayerfully *29*
privilege .... *viii*
prized .... *v*
puzzle *44, 45, 46, 52*
reaching *50*
REALLY *14*
recovery *22*
Recovery *17*
reflect .... *iii, 18*
rejoice *14, 74*
relationships *19, 34, 35, 37, 39, 40, 43, 56*
remain ... *18, 29, 39, 57*

respect................ *ix, 35*
rise.............. *viii, 35, 62*
Sandwich *26*
Satan........................*49*
screaming *13*
screams *13*
Seasons *13*
Serenity....................*30*
share *39, 42, 50, 51, 56, 74*
smile *75*
sometimes... 13, 44, 48, 50, 55
Spirit *vii, 22, 23, 26, 27, 33, 35, 59, 64, 67, 69, 70, 76*
spiritual........*15, 36, 73*
story.............. *ix, 23, 74*
strengthened 13, 66, 74
strong...... *vi, 14, 56, 69*
struggles .... *v, 18, 48*
students....................*43*
study............*18, 23, 36*
suicide..........*30, 51, 61*
Surrender *48, 49*
surrendered *67*
surrounded *32, 34*
Sustainer............. *iii, 63*
Table of Contents...... xi
talk *22*

tears ... *iii, vi, vii, 27, 39, 50, 74, 75*
testimonies.......... *iii, 19*
tethered *36*
thanks......................*14*
tragedies...................*47*
traumatic......*13, 42, 51*
treatments *43*
tribulation *23, 68*
trusts *58*
trustworthy............. *viii*
understand ..*21, 38, 44, 51, 63*
valedictory *59*
village *34*
virus *27, 32, 61*
voice .... *ix, 19, 52*
wait .*29, 37, 56, 59, 61, 65*
waiting..*27, 29, 56, 57, 59, 60, 61, 65*
weary *23, 31, 57, 60, 65, 68, 75*
Winter *13*
witness *23, 35*
word...*v, vii, 31, 35, 36, 38, 44, 47, 52*
words *13, 14, 18, 30, 59, 63, 64*
worship .*31, 35, 39, 66, 73, 80*

www.ingramcontent.com/pod-product-compliance
Lightning Source LLC
Chambersburg PA
CBHW050444010526
44118CB00013B/1669